Beasts and Monsters

Tracey Turner

EDGE FRANKLIN WATTS

LONDON•SYDNEY

First published in 2013 by
Franklin Watts
338 Euston Road
London NW1 3BH

Franklin Watts Australia
Level 17/207 Kent Street
Sydney NSW 2000

Text © Tracey Turner 2013
Design © Franklin Watts 2013

Series editor: Adrian Cole
Art direction: Peter Scoulding
Design: D R Ink
Picture research: Diana Morris

Acknowledgements:
Algol/Shutterstock: 8.
Elle Arden Images/Shutterstock: 17.
Dimitrii Brighidov/istockphoto: front cover.
Linda Bucklin/Shutterstock: 14.
Columbia/Kobal: 19. diversepixel/Shutterstock: 15.
Allen Douglas, www.allendouglasstudio.com: 9.
Fortean/Topfoto: 20. Fortean/Sibbick/Topfoto: 12.
Fotokostic/Shutterstock: 16, 22. Victor Habbick/Shutterstock: 18.
Michael Mowat, www.michaelmowat.carbonmade.com : 6.
Brian Mutschler, www.brianmutschler.com: 11.
Luca Oleastri/Dreamstime: 21. Bob Orsillo/Shutterstock: 7.
Renata Sedmakova/Shutterstock: 5.
Chris Smith, www.chrissmithillustration.com : 23.
Chris Smith, www.chrissmithillustration.com/
Science et Vie Junior n°95: 4. Emma Weakley: 10.
Ben Wootten, www.benwootten.com/ courtesy of Paizo.com: 13.

Every attempt has been made to clear copyright. Should
there be any inadvertent omission please apply to the
publisher for rectification.

A CIP catalogue record for this book
is available from the British Library.

Dewey Classification: 398.2'454

(pb) ISBN: 978 1 4451 1477 4
(Library ebook) ISBN: 978 1 4451 2509 1

Printed in China

Franklin Watts is a division of Hachette
Children's Books, an Hachette UK company.
www.hachette.co.uk

**Warning!
This is not a
normal book!**

Contents

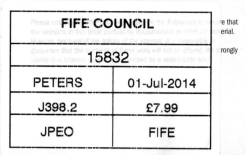

Ultimate 20 is not just a book where you can find out loads of facts and stats about fantastic stuff – it's also a brilliant game book!

How to play

1. Grab a copy of *Ultimate 20* – oh, you have. OK, now get your friends to grab a copy, too.

2. Each player closes their eyes and flicks to a game page. Now, open your eyes and choose one of the Ultimate 20. Decide who goes first, then that person reads out what critter they've chosen, plus the name of the stat. For example, this player has chosen the Hydra and the Strength stat, with an Ultimate 20 ranking of 3.

Strength: **3**
Intelligence: **9**
Speed: **11**
Magic: **9**
Terror rating: **5**
Killer factor: **7**

3. Now, challenge your friends to see who has the highest-ranking stat – the lower the number (from 1–20) the better your chances of winning. (1 = good, 20 = goofy).

Player 1

Strength: **3**

Player 2

Strength: **15**

4. Whoever has the lowest number is the winner – nice one! If you have the same number – you've tied.

Time to flick, choose, challenge again!

(If you land on the same game page, choose the Ultimate 20 listing opposite.)

Mash it up!

If you haven't got the same *Ultimate 20* book as your friends, you can **STILL** play — Ultimate 20 Mash Up! The rules are the same as the regular game (above), so flick and choose one of your Ultimate 20 and a stat, then read out them out. Each player does this. Now read out the Ultimate 20 ranking to see whose choice is the best. Can a McLaren P1 car beat a tank? Can Bobby Charlton beat a king cobra snake?

Yeti

The yeti, also known as the Abominable Snowman, lurks in the Himalayas, a mountain range with the highest peaks on Earth.

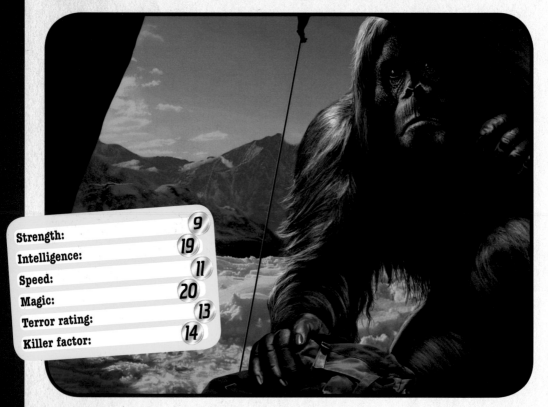

Strength:	9
Intelligence:	19
Speed:	11
Magic:	20
Terror rating:	13
Killer factor:	14

Big and hairy

The Himalayan people have told stories about a great big lumbering hairy creature called a yeti for centuries. Yetis became more widely known in the early and middle part of the 20th century, when Westerners first attempted to climb mountains in the Himalayas. Since then, there have been many reports of a large, ape-like creature, covered in dark hair, high in the mountains. Enormous footprints in the snow have been found – some, discovered in 2007, measured 33 cm long by 25 cm wide. Sadly there's no hard evidence of the creature's existence.

Bigfoot

North America has its own version of the yeti, called Bigfoot or a sasquatch. It has been spotted in Canada and the northwest of the United States. The creature is described as large and hairy, like the yeti, but also extremely stinky. At least you'll smell him coming for you!

Sphinx

In Greek and Egyptian legend, a sphinx was a creature with a lion's body and a human head and torso, and sometimes wings – and one in particular had a habit of eating people!

Theban Sphinx

The most famous sphinx lurked on a rocky cliff outside the city of Thebes, killing and devouring passers-by if they couldn't answer her riddle. The riddle: what has one voice, but becomes four-footed, then two-footed, then three-footed? It was finally answered correctly by Oedipus (who went on to kill his father and marry his mother)*. The Sphinx was so furious that she hurled herself into the sea and died.

Sphinx statues

The ancient Egyptians carved lots of statues of sphinxes. The biggest, known as the Great Sphinx, has the head of an Egyptian pharaoh. It was made around 4,500 years ago and still stands near the pyramids of Giza.

Strength:	15
Intelligence:	5
Speed:	17
Magic:	8
Terror rating:	16
Killer factor:	18

*The answer is a man, who crawls when he's a baby, then walks on two legs, then uses a walking stick when he's old.

Basilisk

The legendary basilisk is a dangerous beast: it is highly venomous, and can kill just by looking at you. So don't look at it!

Rooster snake

The basilisk is king of all snakes, part-snake and part-cockerel. Legend has it that the creature hatches from the egg of a reptile that's been kept warm by a cockerel. Its venom is so toxic that it leaves a trail of poisoned vegetation wherever it goes, and anyone it looks at will die instantly.

Weasels and cockerels

Apparently, there are two ways to kill a basilisk: the smell of a weasel is enough to kill it (though the weasel will die too), and the cry of a cockerel will also cause the basilisk to drop dead. For this reason, travellers in the Middle Ages would sometimes carry a cockerel with them – just in case!

Strength:	4
Intelligence:	10
Speed:	14
Magic:	7
Terror rating:	1
Killer factor:	1

Werewolf

Werewolves are people who change into fearsome wolf-like creatures at full moon, and change back at daybreak.

Becoming a werewolf

There are different ways to become a werewolf: some people are born werewolves (maybe because they're born on Christmas Day, or because they're the seventh son of a seventh son). Others gain the power of transformation from magical objects or potions, while some are victims of a werewolf attack. If a werewolf bites or scratches someone (and they don't die), the victim becomes a werewolf too. However people become werewolves, though, all of them are ferocious and deadly. Legend has it that the only way to kill a werewolf is with a silver weapon, such as a sword or bullet.

Strength:	9
Intelligence:	11
Speed:	10
Magic:	11
Terror rating:	8
Killer factor:	8

The Beast of Gévaudan

The Beast of Gévaudan, in central France, killed perhaps as many as 100 people, and was thought to be a werewolf – there were reports that the beast walked on two legs. Two large wolves were found and shot. Some stories say that silver bullets were used – and the attacks stopped.

http://preview.tinyurl.com/cjtfxfl

Centaur

Centaurs are part-human and part-horse creatures
from Greek mythology, famous for their wild nature.

Wild and unpredictable

In Greek myths centaurs are seen as wild,
drunken, unpredictable and uncivilised.
The most famous story about the centaurs
is their fight with the Lapiths, a legendary
tribe from Thessaly, the region of Greece
where the centaurs lived. The centaurs
gatecrashed the king's wedding and tried
to kidnap the Lapith women, including
the bride. With help from the Greek hero
Theseus, who also killed the bull-monster
the Minotaur, the Lapiths won.

Strength:	15
Intelligence:	7
Speed:	6
Magic:	6
Terror rating:	13
Killer factor:	14

Chiron the Healer

The centaur Chiron was different
from the other, badly behaved
centaurs: he was wise and an
expert healer, and acted as
a tutor to some of the Greek
heroes, including Theseus.

Bunyip

In the legends of the Aboriginal Australians, the bunyip is a terrifying, bone-crunching swamp monster. It breathes air and can leave the water – perhaps in search of its prey, which might well be human beings, especially women and children.

Swamp dweller

Descriptions of the bunyip vary so greatly that they aren't much help if you want to spot one: a giant starfish, a hippo's body with a long neck and round head, a cross between a bird and an alligator, a huge snake with a beard and a mane, and a half-human, half-bird hybrid.

Strength:	5
Intelligence:	14
Speed:	14
Magic:	5
Terror rating:	4
Killer factor:	9

Extinct beast

Some people believe that the bunyip did live in Australia. They think that during the time of the very earliest Australian people – many thousands of years ago – the bunyip was a real animal, and since then it has become extinct.

Kelpie

Kelpies, from Celtic folklore, are water creatures that lure people to a horrible death. They're shape-shifters, but usually take the form of a beautiful white or black horse.

Water horse

Kelpies are found near streams, lakes and rivers in Scotland and Ireland. They seem very friendly, and encourage passing humans – especially children – to jump up onto their backs for a ride. But once somebody climbs on, they become stuck to the kelpie's back. The kelpie then charges off with its human victim, plunges into the deepest part of the water, and drowns and then devours them.

Strength: **19**

Intelligence: **3**

Speed: **4**

Magic: **3**

Terror rating: **16**

Killer factor: **12**

Wet weeds

Spotting a kelpie is tricky. It's best not to go near a friendly looking pony if it's standing on its own near water. The real giveaway is the beast's mane, which will always be dripping wet. Some say that the kelpie's mane is made of water weeds.

The Chimera

The Chimera is a three-headed, fire-breathing monster from Greek mythology. It had three heads: a lion's head, a goat's head (in the middle of its back) and a snake's head (forming the tail).

Bellerophon and Pegasus

The Chimera lived in Lycia, in what's now Turkey, until she was killed by the Greek hero Bellerophon. Bellerophon had the advantage of being airborne, because he'd managed to tame the flying horse, Pegasus. He shot arrows at the Chimera, one of which was tipped with lead and melted in her fiery breath, killing the creature.

Strength:	5
Intelligence:	14
Speed:	11
Magic:	9
Terror rating:	9
Killer factor:	5

Burning gas

In southwest Turkey, on the Lycian Way, gas vents in the ground still burn methane gas, as they have since ancient times. These flaming vents, known as 'chimera' today, are probably why the myth of the monstrous Chimera began.

Chupacabras

'Chupacabras' is a Spanish word meaning 'goat-sucker'. This blood-sucking beast is thought to be responsible for the deaths of farm animals in the Americas and other parts of the world.

Blood-sucker

Reports of dead farm animals, drained of blood with teeth marks in their necks, began in Puerto Rico in 1995. Since then there have been many cases, mostly in Central and South America and the United States, with a few in Russia and the Philippines. People have reported seeing the mysterious chupacabras, describing it as a dog-like reptile, with leathery skin, and sometimes with spines along its back, or red glowing eyes.

Wily coyotes

Several times, what's thought to be a chupacabras has been shot and killed. In almost all these cases, the creature has turned out to be a coyote, or another animal in the dog family, with a severe case of mange.

Strength:	7
Intelligence:	14
Speed:	6
Magic:	15
Terror rating:	5
Killer factor:	11

Kraken

The Kraken is the biggest and most terrifying sea monster of all. Tales of this ferocious beast have scared sailors in northern oceans for centuries.

Huge and deadly

The Kraken, found in Scandinavian seas, is described as an enormous, tentacled squid or octopus, which is so huge it could reach up to the top of the mast on a sailing ship. According to legend, the Kraken is so massive that some sailors thought it was an island. When they got too close it rose up and smashed their ship. Then the Kraken drowned and ate the sailors.

Scary squid

Many stories were told of ships lost because of attacks by the fearsome Kraken. Perhaps the monster is based on giant deep-sea squid, which have long tentacles covered in suckers full of sharp, gripping teeth. The biggest giant squid ever recorded was 18.5 m long and weighed nearly 1,000 kg. Giant squid have been known to fight sperm whales, and win.

Strength:	1
Intelligence:	15
Speed:	3
Magic:	11
Terror rating:	1
Killer factor:	4

Gorgon

The Gorgons of Greek legend are three unbelievably ugly sisters. They had a writhing mass of live snakes on their heads instead of hair. Just one look at their hideous faces would turn you to stone.

Medusa and Perseus

The hero Perseus was given the difficult task of cutting off a Gorgon's head – two of the Gorgons were immortal but one, Medusa, could die. Luckily, Perseus had help from a goddess, who gave him a mirrored shield. He used it to look at the horribly ugly creature's reflection, rather than directly at her. He chopped Medusa's head off without being turned to stone, put it in a bag he'd brought specially, and flew off on his winged sandals. Even the chopped-off head was capable of turning anyone who looked at it to stone.

Strength:	15
Intelligence:	7
Speed:	18
Magic:	11
Terror rating:	5
Killer factor:	3

Gorgon blood

When Perseus killed Medusa the Gorgon, the flying horse Pegasus sprang from her blood – and went on to help Bellerophon kill the Chimera.

Dragon

Strength:	2
Intelligence:	1
Speed:	6
Magic:	2
Terror rating:	12
Killer factor:	6

Dragons are enormous, fire-breathing, flying reptiles. People have told stories about them for centuries in many different parts of the world.

Dragon slayers

In Europe, dragons look like giant lizards with wings, and in Russia they usually have three heads. Dragons are fond of eating people or imprisoning young women, and they often need to be dealt with by a hero. Perhaps the most famous dragonslayer is Saint George. He killed a dragon that had been feasting upon the people of Silene, just as it was about to eat the king's daughter.

Chinese dragons

Chinese dragons are more snake-like than European ones, and usually have four legs and no wings, although they can still fly. Unlike European dragons, they control rain, rivers, lakes and seas. They are wise and kind, and are a symbol of power – when China was an empire, the Emperor's emblem was a dragon.

Hydra

The fearsome Hydra is the poisonous, water-dwelling, many-headed monster of Greek legend. The Hydra lived in Lake Lerna, guarding an entrance to the Underworld that lay beneath the water.

Deadly breath

The Hydra had a snake-like body and many heads – ranging from three to nine. Its breath was poisonous, and could kill with just one whiff!

Impossible task

The Greek hero Heracles was set 12 impossible-sounding labours by the gods, as a punishment. One task was to kill the Hydra. Heracles covered his mouth and nose to protect himself from the Hydra's breath, and began chopping off its heads – but every time the hero hacked one off, two new heads grew in its place!

Team effort

Heracles finally defeated the Hydra with the help of his nephew Iolaus: every time Heracles chopped off a head, Iolaus sealed up the stump with a red-hot poker, so that no new heads could grow.

Strength:	3
Intelligence:	9
Speed:	11
Magic:	9
Terror rating:	5
Killer factor:	7

Unicorn

Unlike most of the Ultimate 20 beasts, the legendary one-horned horse isn't at all scary and is very unlikely to eat you. Unicorns are beautiful horses – usually white – with a single spiral horn in the middle of their foreheads. They could only be tamed by young women.

Goodness and purity

Unicorns appear in ancient stories from India, China and the Middle East, and became especially popular in Europe during the Middle Ages. Unicorns became a symbol of love, goodness and purity.

Magic horn

A unicorn's horn is supposed to have magic powers to cure disease and make poisoned water drinkable. Anyone who drinks from a unicorn's horn is protected from disease, and so unicorn-horn cups were very highly prized during the Middle Ages. The cups weren't really made from unicorn's horns, of course, but from the horn of a rhinoceros or a narwhal – a single-horned Arctic sea creature.

Strength:	18
Intelligence:	2
Speed:	6
Magic:	1
Terror rating:	19
Killer factor:	19

Loch Ness Monster

There have been reports of a monster in the dark, deep waters of Loch Ness, in Scotland, since the Dark Ages (c.500–1000CE). The earliest recorded one was in 565 CE. However, most sightings were reported in the 20th century.

Prehistoric plesiosaur

Recent sightings of the Loch Ness Monster – or 'Nessie' – often included photographs people had taken of the beast. People describe Nessie as huge and dark-coloured, with a long neck much like a plesiosaur, a prehistoric water creature which is supposed to have died out 70 million years ago!

Strength: **11**
Intelligence: **16**
Speed: **5**
Magic: **16**
Terror rating: **13**
Killer factor: **16**

Photo opportunity

Photographs of the Loch Ness Monster are not clear enough to prove its existence. The loch has also been scanned using sonar, but again the evidence is not conclusive. Perhaps people have mistaken seals or driftwood for a monster – or maybe Nessie is very good at hide-and-seek...

Cyclops

The cyclops are a race of man-eating giants from Greek and Roman legend. Each cyclops has a single eye in the middle of his forehead.

Odysseus and the cyclops

The best known story about the cyclops is from an ancient Greek poem called *The Odyssey*. The ferocious cyclops lived on a remote island, where they kept sheep. The Greek hero Odysseus arrived on the island. Unfortunately, Odysseus and his men found themselves inside the cave of a cyclops called Polyphemus. The cyclops killed several men by removing their brains, then eating them. Odysseus sharpened one of the giant's huge clubs and blinded him with it, and escaped with his men (at least, the ones who hadn't been eaten).

Zeus's thunderbolts

In another ancient Greek story, the cyclops are three brothers who forge metal objects and make the thunderbolts hurled by Zeus, the king of the gods.

Strength:	7
Intelligence:	20
Speed:	14
Magic:	16
Terror rating:	11
Killer factor:	13

Mongolian Death Worm

In the remote Gobi Desert, the fearsome Mongolian Death Worm lies in wait – or so many people believe. There the beast is called *allghoi khorkhoi*, or 'intestine worm', because it looks like a piece of animal intestine – red, rubbery and horrible.

Horror worm

The Mongolian Death Worm is 1–1.5 m long, and lives underground – venturing out to capture its prey. The worm is so poisonous that anyone who touches it dies instantly. The monster can also spurt lethal acid, and is capable of creating an electric charge that can knock down a horse. Many stories are told of the Death Worm killing and eating people – particularly children.

Strength:	14
Intelligence:	17
Speed:	19
Magic:	16
Terror rating:	1
Killer factor:	1

Death Worm expeditions

There have been several expeditions to track down the Mongolian Death Worm. So far, no one has proved the creature's existence, but many Mongolian people believe the deadly creature is absolutely real.

Mothman

Sightings of a weird, red-eyed bird-man terrified the people of West Virginia, USA, in the 1960s. It didn't attack, but it did scare them!

Batman

The first sighting of Mothman was by five men working in a cemetery. They spotted a large man-like creature with wings as it flew over their heads. A few days later, there were reports of a similar creature, more than 2 m tall with glowing red eyes, which flew after a car. The creature became known as Mothman, after a character from a Batman TV series.

Strength:	13
Intelligence:	9
Speed:	2
Magic:	14
Terror rating:	14
Killer factor:	16

Bridge disaster

Sightings of the red-eyed flying man continued, as well as reports of Unidentified Flying Objects (UFOs), until 1967 when a road bridge over the Ohio River collapsed, killing 46 people. After the tragedy, sightings stopped. Some people believe that the events are connected, but Mothman remains a mystery.

Phoenix

The beautiful phoenix is a legendary bird famous for being reborn from the ashes of a fire. Only one phoenix exists at any one time – it's about the size of an eagle, with red and gold feathers.

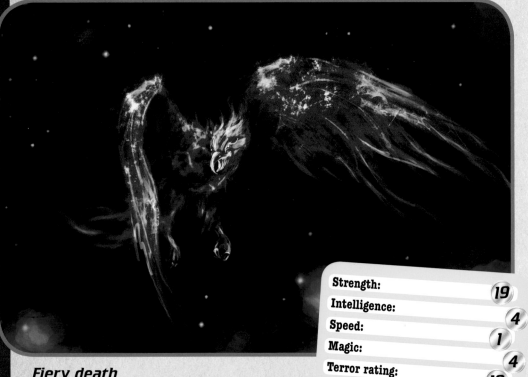

Strength:	19
Intelligence:	4
Speed:	1
Magic:	4
Terror rating:	19
Killer factor:	19

Fiery death

The phoenix lives for at least 500 years, then, when it senses it's about to die, it builds itself a nest at the top of an oak tree, using cinnamon and myrrh. The bird sets fire to the nest and dies, but a new bird is born from the ashes. It flies with the old phoenix's ashes to the altar of the god of the sun, and leaves them there.

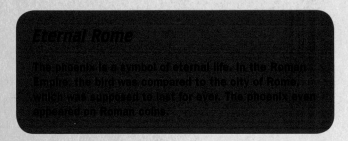

Eternal Rome

The phoenix is a symbol of eternal life. In the Roman Empire, the bird was compared to the city of Rome, which was supposed to last for ever. The phoenix even appeared on Roman coins.

Mokèlé Mbèmbé

This huge and fearsome beast lurks in the lakes and rivers of the Congo River Basin in Africa. The Mokèlé Mbèmbé, which means 'one who stops the flow of rivers', is an enormous creature – up to 10 m long – with a very long neck and tail.

Prehistoric plant eater

Eyewitnesses describe it as similar to a sauropod dinosaur. It lives mainly near or under water, venturing out to eat the malombo plant. Although it's a herbivore (it eats only veggies), there are claims that the Mokèlé Mbèmbé has killed people by overturning their boats and biting them or lashing out with its long tail.

Strength:	11
Intelligence:	18
Speed:	20
Magic:	19
Terror rating:	5
Killer factor:	9

Hunting the Mokèlé Mbèmbé

There have been sightings of the beast for hundreds of years and many expeditions have been mounted to find it. The most recent was in 2011 and was shown on the National Geographic Channel – but so far no one has managed to prove the creature's existence.

Glossary

Celtic – relating to the Celts, a people who lived in areas of Europe including Ireland, Scotland and Wales

driftwood – pieces of wood which are drifting out at sea or have been washed ashore

eternal – lasting forever

extinct – when a group of animals dies out

folklore – legends, traditions and beliefs, often recorded in stories and music

immortal – living forever

intestines – the internal part of an animal's body which stretches between the stomach and the anus

legendary – relating to a story from ancient times

mange – a disease that causes hair loss in animals

myrrh – a sticky plant substance used in perfumes and medicines

mythology – a collection of stories belonging to a particular time or place

sauropod – the largest of the dinosaur groups, they were four-legged with a long neck and tail, and only ate plants

sonar – a machine that can detect objects underwater

Underworld – the underground kingdom where the ancient Greeks believed that the souls of people went after death

venomous – an animal that can give a poisonous bite or sting

Index